Fr Timothy Radci
interviewed by Raymc

Friday 30 October 2015 at Blackfriars, Oxford

RF: Fr Timothy, thank you for the warm welcome to Blackfriars — it's good to be with you. Can I ask you, first of all please, just to share with us something about your own background in the faith, the Catholic culture you were brought up in, maybe some early influences in your life?

TR: I think that faith was very pervasive of my childhood. My parents were very committed believers but we weren't at all pious. We did have one attempt at family rosary but it broke down when the dogs burst in and started licking us! I think one of the most important things I'd say, for me, was friendship. I had a great uncle who was a Benedictine, my Great Uncle Dick, and you had a tremendous sense of a man who was a friend of God, and we had friendship with the monks and the religious and the priests who came to stay. We even thought of the saints as our friends, so there was none of this gloomy Catholic guilt that everybody talks about. I never encountered that at all. So the faith of my childhood was relaxed, joyful.

> one of the most important things… was friendship

RF: You mentioned the Benedictine connection to the family, yet you became a Dominican so what drew you to the Dominicans?

TR: I didn't know any Dominicans when I decided to join the order, which may have been just as well really. What drew me to the order was the motto, Truth – *Veritas*. When I was at school with the Benedictine's, I actually wasn't at all a pious boy; I was always smoking and trying to get to the nearest pub and I was almost expelled for reading *Lady Chatterley's Lover* during Benediction, so I wasn't the sort of boy who imagined being a priest from an early age. When I left school I made friends with people who weren't Christian and they said "It isn't true; what you believe is not true" and that became an obsessive question: "Is it true"? And I began to think "If it is true, it must be important". Then I remember there was a religious order which had the motto "Truth", but I couldn't remember which order, so I contacted the Benedictines and they told me it was the Dominicans and here I am fifty years later.

I actually wasn't at all a pious boy

So I was really drawn by the whole idea of truth. When I visited the novitiate and had my first weekend staying with the order, I suppose what attracted me was the humanity of the brothers. I arrived from London wearing my suit and tie, a rather 'Downton Abbey' sort of person, and there were these two friars, quite young, wearing old duffel coats and jeans. We went to the pub and one had a sense of immense freedom. One could talk about anything and I felt "this is life and it could be a life for me."

RF: The idea of truth is a very interesting one. Is that something you feel you've found or is it a lifelong journey? Is truth the same as certainty, because a lot of people on the Christian journey struggle sometimes with certainty and there seems to be gaps in people's faith and uncertainty? Have you found truth after all these years?

TR: When I was a young friar, full of enthusiasm, I had quite a naïve idea of truth. I thought, 'there it is, I've got it, I've got it sorted now'. But the longer I stayed in the order, the longer I studied, the longer that I meditated over scripture, the more that I tried to grapple with the truths of our faith, the more I found, in fact, you're always drawn to a mystery which is beyond our words and so there's plenty of room for questioning, for doubting, for searching. In fact, the moment you stop searching, in a way, you lose it. So I would say that the commitment to truth remains central to my vocation, but now I realise that the fullness of truth is always to be found. One is on a journey and you

the fullness of truth is always to be found

need the help of your friends, you need the help of people with other faiths and with no faith as you try to draw near to something which escapes our words in the end.

RF: What's your understanding of mystery? I think it was Rahner who described God as the holy mystery? Is mystery something we're kind of clueless before? How would you help us understand the idea of mystery or the mystery of God?

TR: Sometimes we think mystery is simply something which is incomprehensible, "It's a mystery what has happened to so many of my socks", for example. But for a Christian, a mystery is not simply something that I cannot understand. Rather it is a truth which is so filled with meaning, so radiantly fascinating, that it escapes our words. St Thomas Aquinas said that in this life we're joined to God as to the unknown. It's not that God is somehow dark, but rather a light which blinds.

God is… a light which blinds

RF: And that, presumably, is what helps us to trust the mysteries. We're not being led astray, we're not being led down a blind alley.

TR: Absolutely. It's not as if our Christian doctrine is a bizarre teaching. All our doctrines are about the incomprehensible mystery of the utter love that God has for us and it's a love which is always beyond our grasp. St Augustine said "God is always more" so you're always at the edge of understanding what it might be to be so loved.

RF: If we could go back to the Dominicans for a moment. Could you just describe your understanding of the charism of the Dominican order and what it has to offer today's world? I think you wrote somewhere recently that you predict a revival of religious life which happens every... I think you said every couple of hundred years. So, the Dominicans after 800 years, which is a long time – what do they have to offer today's world and on what grounds do you predict a revival of the religious orders generally?

TR: First of all, at the fount of our Dominican tradition stand two great and very different people and I think our charism is interplayed between them. There is St Dominic, who's out in the fields, he's out in the streets, and he's encountering people, engaging them

> ... he had an "open-eyed spirituality"

in conversation and debate. One of my brethren said he had an "open-eyed spirituality"; he's touched by the suffering of the poor and sells all his books to raise money for them. So he's very experiential, he's immersed in the world. And then there is St Thomas Aquinas who is an academic and he's reflecting on it all, he's trying to make sense of everything in the light of his faith. I think that the Dominican tradition is strongest when there is an interplay between the people out there, immersed in the stream of life, and the thinkers and scholars who reflect upon the experience of the brethren on the street, study the scriptures and the tradition. The truth needs both. It must be lived and reflected upon.

> When we have… lived experience and deep reflection, we thrive.

If we just had the academics, our idea of the faith would be abstract and lifeless, if we just had those immersed in the busyness of life, then our grasp of the truth might be superficial. When we have both of these, lived experience and deep reflection, we thrive. So in the sixteenth century Bartolomé de Las Casas, the first person in European history to oppose all slavery, was out there in the Americas, fighting for the rights of the indigenous people, recording their sufferings. In Spain, in the University of Salamanca, Francisco de Vitoria read Las Casas' works, reflected on their implication and he evolved the first theory of international human rights, due to every human being. Crucial was the interplay between them, the friar on the spot and the thinker in the library. They dialogued, and didn't always agree. Or in the twentieth century there was the Worker Priest Movement, priests immersed in the world of work, labouring in factories and their guru was a wonderful man I knew very well called Marie-Dominique Chenu. He was often called the grandfather of the Vatican Council. So in our own English province we have our theologians and we've got brethren who are working in the parishes and often with the poor. The important thing is that they listen to each other because the truth in its fullness needs both.

And then, Raymond, you asked about the future of religious life. First of all I'm confident because every couple of hundred years there have been revivals of religious life in unexpected ways. At the beginning of the thirteenth century, religious life was still largely monastic, cloistered in great abbeys, far from the flux and energy of the new towns and universities. No one would have expected the explosion of a new way of being religious, the friars such as the Franciscans, Dominicans and the Carmelites. Then with the Renaissance and Reformation, there are new orders, such as the Jesuits and the Capuchins and the Ursulines, responding to new challenges of a new world. And then in the late eighteenth/nineteenth century there is an explosion of new religious orders coping with the new industrial world, the new poverty on the edges of these great cities. So I'm confident that religious life will be renewed. The Church needs it.

> I'm confident that religious life will be renewed.

RF: What would attract young people, or would it be young people? When I was a young man I went to junior seminary; I felt some calling to vocation and that vocation has developed in different ways. What would attract anybody, but especially young people, to devote themselves to religious orders in this day and age?

TR: Because I think young people want to do something crazy. I think if we try and attract young people by offering a comfortable, unchallenging secure life, then they will not come, or at least not the ones whom we need! Whereas if we say to people "Come and join us and do something mad for God", I think people will respond, because young people are immensely generous. Young people want adventure. If we try to sell Christianity as something nice and safe – light a candle and find where you are on the Enneagram – they'll be bored, whereas if we challenge people to give away their lives, then they may be excited. And religious life *is* reviving. Just to take the Dominicans, one in six of all Dominicans in the world are in formation – that's to say in the first five or six years of their religious life. We are attracting young people in the West too, not just in the developing world.

Young people want adventure.

RF: I think you've written somewhere else about wanting the Church to be more courageous, I think you wanted the

Church to be a school of courage and wanted it to be more counter-cultural. Can the Church, should the Church, tap into what's happening in some strains of the secular world which is a kind of counter-cultural movement? Is that another reason why it's a good time to take this step into religious life?

TR: Absolutely, you see there's a tension which is at the heart of Christianity which is fascinating and that is, we have to be both inculturated and counter-cultural. Jesus was a first-century Jew. God became flesh and by being immersed in the culture and humanity of that time and place, God was incarnated as one of us. But Jesus was also counter-cultural, challenging assumptions of his time, not obeying the law, eating with sinners. So in the person of Jesus one sees inculturation and also counter-culturation. That's the challenge for religious life too, we have to be both and I see, as I travel around the world, how religious life has that challenge in the West, in Eastern Europe, in Asia and Africa. We have to become truly African Dominicans, Vietnamese Dominicans, French Dominicans and so on. But also we have to find ways of challenging our societies. In Africa the big challenge is how we challenge the tribalism that sometimes pervades African society; in the West we need a way of life that both recognises what it

> God was incarnated as one of us

is like to be a modern individual, but which also challenges the extreme individualism of our society. And of course the difficulty is that one person's inculturation is another person's counter-culturation and this is where disagreement is likely to occur. I might think that inculturation means having a car and a bank account, someone else might think that is succumbing to the consumerist society.

RF: And I suppose it's about being true to the Gospel, isn't it? You mentioned our inspiring figure, our Lord, this first century Jew who was so counter-cultural, a very attractive figure and you've spoken about this before. Is it the case, if we turn our attention to the Church or the institutional Church, if you like, if at the heart of the Church is this very attractive figure, why are more people not drawn to that figure or the Church? Is the Church sometimes an obstacle in getting to know or getting close to Jesus, our Lord and Saviour?

TR: Yes, and it has been from the beginning. Right from the beginning you see this ambiguity. On the one hand, the Church attracts people to this man who said "I will draw all things to myself", on the other hand, from the beginning Jesus chose a pretty rum bunch of people. I mean, he chose Judas, who betrayed him, he chose Peter who denied him, he chose Simon the zealot who was probably some sort of revolutionary; he chose James and John who were into power and wanting to get ahead of everybody else and rule the roost. Either we see the weakness, the fallibility, of the Church as an obstacle, or we see it as a sign that God, from the beginning, chose people who were weak and sometimes sinful and stupid. These are the ones he wanted, he didn't look around and say 'Let's find the most impressive people we've got', he chose ordinary weak people and that's a sign that we're all welcome, we can all find a place in this Church because he chose those whom St Paul said were not of noble birth, who are not highly educated, just very ordinary.

> we can all find a
> place in this Church

RF: From the beginning we've been arguing about what we believe, right back to the Council of Jerusalem in AD 50 or whatever it was, we've been having rows about what to believe in, right down to the present day, we have the synod on the family and discussions about what we believe in and can that evolve and can it change. For a Christian today, what do you believe is the most important thing? Pope Francis seems to be trying to get us back to the essence, the core, the kerygma, the proclamation, but we've always had the didache, the teaching. Is it important to believe everything about the Catholic Church to be a Catholic, or is it more important to hold on to the core, to the essence of faith?

TR: You have to start, obviously, as Pope Francis says, with the core of the Gospel, that God so utterly loves us that he has shared our life, defeated hatred and death – that's the essence. Nothing that we say must get in the way of that and sometimes the way we've taught doctrine has done this. It's complexity has put people off. So I think that Pope Francis is summoning us back to 'That without which it's all incomprehensible'. But I think when you understand the doctrines of the Church all right, they always help us to understand what it means to be loved. So, for example, the Church teaches the divinity of Christ. A lot of people might say 'Oh, that really makes things complicated. We don't need to bother about that. Stick with the nice man who wandered around Galilee'. But properly understood, the fact that it was truly God embracing us, actually helps us to understand how wonderful is this love that God has for us. He loved us so much as to become one of us. All the great doctrines of the Church help us to understand the core of the Gospel,

He loved us so much as to become one of us.

but you have to start with the core, otherwise you won't be able to see why that's the case. You don't want to make a belief checklist – you only belong if you tick all the boxes – that would put people in terrible mental torture, but I do believe that ultimately all the doctrines of the faith illuminate the central mystery of God's great love.

RF: If we could just pick up on those very interesting points. I'm thinking, and a lot of people have been thinking after the synod, about those people who might feel unloved in the Church or by the Church, and people whose sexuality, for example, feels to them as if they are different, or some of the language the Church might have used in the past is quite cold, quite harsh and they don't feel very loved, or perhaps they're divorced and feel excluded. How would you help people who are struggling with those doctrines, with that teaching, who personally feel unloved or who feel that the teaching of the Church is not very loving?

TR: First of all you just have to be with them. Often we talk about people who are divorced and remarried, we talk about gay people. The first thing, if we want to have a Church that is really welcoming, is to talk with them and that means listening to them with all our intelligence and sympathy. It means believing that they have something to teach us. I've often been moved by talking with men and women who have been divorced and remarried and what they've lived through and what they've suffered and how they've struggled and so instead of seeing their situation as a problem to be solved, we should see them as people who have wisdom to give us. We won't find our way forward until we listen to them. It's the same with people who are gay. They're not a problem, "What are we going to do about all these gay people?" They are our friends and we must listen to what they can teach us if we are going to be able to teach them. The Church has authority when she gives authority to what other people experience.

You see, anybody who loves, in any way, whether it's a love of husband and wife, or fraternal love in a religious community or the love of your children, or of two people in any relationship, wherever there's love, then we have something to learn. We have to give authority for what people have lived and what they've learned. There was a Bishop of Limerick, who, a long time ago, gave what he thought was a wonderful talk about sex and as he walked down the aisle he overheard two women in front of him and one said "What another wonderful talk by the Bishop about sex" and the other one said "Yes, it's just as well he doesn't know as much about it as we do." So a disciple is someone who is always learning. That's what the word means. We learn by listening to the Word of God and we learn as we study the tradition, but we also learn as we listen to people and what they live.

a disciple is someone who is always learning

RF: Do you see a shift in the Church's behaviour in that respect? The synod seems to be listening more; there were those questionnaires prior to the synod, and that was different from the Vatican Council when there wasn't a safe degree of consultation. Is that something you see as a genuine shift for the future that you see a new pattern there, initiated by Pope Francis?

TR: Yes. For Pope Francis central for the renewal of the Church is conversation. He founded the C9, the nine cardinals with whom he has conversations about what is on his heart. And he wants the synod to become conversational, which means that you speak and you listen. I took part in three synods and they weren't very conversational; everybody arrived with their set texts, which they'd written at home, and they read them out aloud, regardless of what anybody else had said. Pope Benedict already tried to move the synod to being more dialogical.

Good conversations are unpredictable

Good conversations are unpredictable, you don't know quite where they're going to go. If you try to control a conversation it goes dead. Pope Francis believes that the working of the Holy Spirit in our lives is always a bit unpredictable, you don't know whence it comes and where it goes, as St John says. So he's trying to get us to open ourselves to the unpredictability of the Spirit. I think Pope Benedict laid down the theological foundation for this understanding of the role of the Spirit in the life of the Church. That is why it is so mistaken to think that there is a fundamental opposition between Benedict and Francis.

Benedict gave us the theology but Francis is putting it into action.

RF: Probably there are those in the Church who would say, with great respect, that there's not a lot of point in having a conversation because nothing's going to change in terms of, we have the Church teaching, Church teaching is permanent, is fixed, so you can have a conversation but nothing's going to change as a result of it. Is that an overly simplistic view? Can you imagine a conversation actually ends up with changing your point of view because of what you've learned in the conversation?

TR: I hope so. I mean the Church frequently lives through death and resurrection. The Church after the Council of Trent was very different from the medieval Church and the Church after the nineteenth century, the first Vatican Council, was very different from the Church of Trent. It entered that new modern industrialised world. Again the Church was radically transformed at the second Vatican Council. That doesn't mean that suddenly all the doctrines are up for grabs, but it does mean that as a community we make further steps in the journey to the truth and, as all the great mystics have known, for example

> the Church frequently lives through death and resurrection.

St Catherine of Siena and Teresa of Avila, whenever you journey towards God you go through moments of darkness and moments of light.

The Church is on a pilgrimage. This means that our doctrines will never be rejected. We shall never as a Church go back on Chalcedon and deny the divinity of Christ. But these doctrines will, as Cardinal Newman said, be developed. And if you don't develop them they die. Karl Rahner talked about what he called 'the heresy of dead orthodoxy'. If you've got it all sorted, you don't have to think any more, but that is the death of the tradition. Fidelity to the tradition means that you go on searching.

RF: Have you had any conversations with Pope Francis, any personal experience of the current pope?

TR: Yes, I've been blessed; I've met him three times. The first time was when he was Archbishop of Buenos Aires and I was already immensely touched by him, his spontaneity, his freedom. And then about eighteen months ago I was very privileged to have a long conversation with him alone; he invited me to come and have a chat and what I found really astonishing is he never looked at his watch. If you meet a lot of people – when I was Master of the Order there'd be whole queues of people – you are inclined discreetly to look at your watch and try to bring a conversation to an end. He never did that. I had a sense that he was determined there would be no control of the conversation, how long or what form it should take, and that gave me enormous freedom. He made me at home. Renunciation of control is a very important part of his whole way of being. And then thirdly I met him briefly when I was in Rome for a dialogue between Christians and Muslims a few months ago.

RF: Has he said anything memorable to you that you'd like to share?

TR: I'm a great believer in respecting confidentiality. I think he deserves to be able to open his heart to somebody and know that they're going to keep it to themselves.

RF: He'll respect your tact, I'm sure. If we could just broaden out the conversation again, perhaps? You've mentioned in your writing the big attraction of the evangelical movements and Pentecostal churches as drawing people away from the Catholic Church. Could you just speak to that, please, and just help us understand what's happening there, and why people, especially in South America and Africa, are being drawn away from the Catholic Church and what it is that they're finding, perhaps, in the Pentecostal churches they're not finding in the Catholic Church.

TR: Two things: First of all, the Pentecostal churches offer the experience of an encounter with the Lord. It is a powerful experience of the Spirit. Our parish worship can all be a bit routine and dull, and you don't really sort of feel that anything much is happening. But in these big Pentecostal assemblies, there is a powerful experience of the Spirit. That attracts people. But the difficulty is this: What happens when the experience stops? You cannot remain

> What happens when the experience stops?

on a high forever! And so there is a pattern which you can see everywhere of people who are converted from Catholicism to some Pentecostal group and then after a while become atheists. They say yesterday's Catholic might become today's Protestant and tomorrow's atheist. If you put so much emphasis on a powerful experience, what have you got when it fades?

It's like with marriage; when you get married, not that I've ever been married, it can be a powerful experience of romantic love, full of excitement, and tenderness, lots of sex! This is wonderful, but in the end a marriage can't endure on just that basis, there has to be a lot of quiet work of establishing profound friendship which may not be terribly romantic. A love that endures involves making meals and accepting that its my turn to take out the rubbish and go to the supermarket! If we don't discover that routine, un-dramatic, quiet love, then love collapses.

So we Catholics must recognise that people need to feel powerfully the presence of God in their lives and the Pentecostals have something to teach us there, but we also have something to offer them, which is a tradition of quiet and enduring spirituality. God is present in the ordinary too. I see people who come to Mass every day here at Blackfriars, day after day. Nothing dramatic happens, the priest doesn't speak in tongues or heal anyone, but a deep transformation, an enduring transformation of our heart and mind happens. This requires persistent, long term devotion of an un-dramatic form. I think that's what we offer. It may seem boring, but a lot of genuine loving involves doing boring things, like washing up and mowing the lawn!

The second thing that these Pentecostal churches offer is the intimacy of belonging, particularly the small churches. You can go along and have your say and you know you're heard and I think that's an important need, to know that you're heard! Your voice should count. For that we have to develop more small groups in the Catholic Church. They can be traditional ones like lay fraternities and guilds, they can be new ones. The Church has always been very inventive, imagining

Your voice should count.

new forms of association. For example there are the teams of Our Lady for married couples. S Egidio in Rome is a movement of lay people working with the poor. Everywhere I go I meet the Focolare movement with its lay spirituality. In all these groups people have a face and a voice. They offer a warm home in the Church which not everyone finds in the anonymity of the parish.

RF: Can we just go back to that wonderful idea of this deep transformation because, at this moment in the Church, it seems to me a very important point. There are many people who were perhaps brought up in the Catholic faith who have got a lot of prayers and devotions, who don't always bring them with them into adult life, or if they do bring them into adult life they cease to make sense and they cease to help them to develop an adult faith and some of the movements I've become aware of, like the centering prayer or rediscovery of the contemplative tradition, seem to be answering that need for inner transformation. Could you just help us to understand how, in the middle of the world we live in, busy people, who are married, or whatever, we can actually set out on that path of transformation and how can the Catholic Church help us to become adult followers of Jesus who are actually on a path of transformation?

TR: I think the busier you are, the more you've got to do, the more it's important that you take time to do nothing.

There's a new generation of young people who are being formed in that quiet spirituality. In Ireland, in many schools, beginning in Dublin, young children are being taught to meditate. Often it is suggested that one needs one minute of silence for every year of your life; when you're ten you have ten minutes of meditation; by the time you're 15 you are able to enjoy a quarter of an hour, and so you slowly acquire the habit of quietness in the presence of the Lord. That's absolutely vital because we often think of prayer as us talking to God but we don't always let God speak to us! It's important that we have moments every day where we linger with God because God may have something to say to us! God may have a challenge for me or a word of assurance or an expression of love. We need times when we are at God's beck and call. It's part of any friendship, isn't it, that you attend to what your friend says, and I think it's true of our divine friendship too. For me that has to be first thing in the morning. I get up early and that's when I can find the time to go and sit and be with God. Often my mind is entirely vacant and that's okay too. Just wait and see what happens.

RF: Where does, to go right back to the beginning, our study come into that, and particularly study of scripture, which the Vatican Council seems to encourage greatly and we had a lot of popular scripture study following that and it seems perhaps to have fallen away a little bit. What's the role of our reading and our study and our reading of the Gospels and scripture, is that still important or is the key just to listen and be contemplative?

TR: We need both. I taught scripture here at Blackfriars for fourteen years and it was the best thing that ever happened to me. I spent months studying the Word of God. I've been a priest now for 44 years, and I'm still astonished all the time by what the Gospels say. You'd have thought by now I would have sussed it. But I go on being surprised and the more that you study, the more you grapple with the details of the text, the more you let the scriptures challenge you, the richer they show themselves to be. But there are other moments when one does not study the text so much as just listen to it, as one listens to a friend.

The temptation is to regard the Word of God as being ammunition in support of what I believe; God's right because God agrees with me. Whereas when you read the scriptures you have to let them challenge you.

> when you read the scriptures you have to let them challenge you.

It becomes exciting when the Word of God says something that you didn't expect, something that you don't want to hear. We really only encounter the scriptures as God's Word to us when they disconcert us. St Dominic wanted us to be beggars and not just begging our bread. More importantly, we should beg for the truth. Often I think when I am preparing a sermon or a lecture I have to rush away and pray but I do not understand what it is all about. 'Give me insight, give me light' and that's when you begin to get somewhere because if you think that you are a great master who knows it all, then you will just bore people, imposing on them your agenda.

RF: Staying with scripture, at the heart of the Gospel is the Passion Narrative and the death and the resurrection of Jesus. Just thinking back to the Pentecostals and the experience of evangelicals, they seem very confident to say publicly Jesus is my personal Lord and Saviour, which a lot of people in the Catholic Church seem to struggle with and in my conversations with Catholics, they often struggle to express what the death of Jesus means for them and what salvation means. We've been taught certain formulas but when you ask people to try and articulate it themselves they seem to struggle with it, and I certainly struggle with it. So can you try and help us with that? – It's quite a big question! What does it mean, what does this terrible, violent death of Jesus mean? Was it atonement to a Father who needed blood to restore relations with humanity or, there are other traditions, aren't there, in the Church that see it slightly differently, so could you help us with that please?

TR: It's fascinating. In Matthew and Mark what you see in Jesus' passion is desolation. But in Luke and John his death is more peaceful. It's the enthronement of Jesus on the cross. For John especially the crucifixion is Jesus' ascent into glory. Two very different stories but you need them both. In Mark and Matthew, we see how God embraces all that's most desolate; there is no dark place in our lives in which God hasn't been present, hasn't shared, hasn't experienced. So the desolation, I think, of the cross in those two gospels expresses a very profound truth; God has embraced even the absence of God. "My God, my God, why have you abandoned me?"

> God has embraced even the absence of God.

But Luke and John's Gospel tell another story which is also true and also necessary which is that Jesus triumphed on the cross. He overcame death and refused to be enslaved by it. This is our own experience when we face suffering and illness and death. Sometimes it can just feel like desolation then we need to read Matthew and Mark and know that God has shared all we suffer. But we also need to find a moment to read John and Luke, and we see that a victory has been won and this is ours too.

RF: For many years the Church seemed to concentrate more on Good Friday than Easter Sunday perhaps, but recently we've been reminded of Easter Sunday and resurrection. What is the significance of resurrection for us as Christians? Is that something you're glad we've rediscovered?

TR: Yes, particularly in Latin America, they put the big stress on Good Friday. If you go to Lima, if you go to most countries in Latin America, Good Friday is the most important day of the year, because they need to believe that God has shared the sufferings they have today. But the extraordinary thing, I think, about Easter Sunday, is not that we've put Good Friday behind us, but as the Early Fathers said, the dead wood of the cross flowers, hatred is defeated, life wins over death. Easter Sunday for me, is the incredible creativity of God. From all that's most barren and sterile and terminal, God brings new life. And I can look at my own life and face what I have done, all that has been sterile and futile and mortal. But the dead wood of my life can flourish too.

In Chile they cover the cross with flowers and then on Easter Sunday they raise it up as if the cross, like a rose bush, has come to blossom again. On Maundy Thursday Jesus bore all that destroyed community: misunderstanding, cowardice, fear, suffering and ultimately death. These are things that divide us from each other and Easter Sunday is the defeat of all that, so now the barriers are down, the barriers have collapsed. "He has destroyed the wall of enmity", Paul says in Ephesians, so that nothing can come between us and God any longer.

RF: You mentioned Maundy Thursday and I know you've written extensively and spoken about it, the last supper and the Eucharist. Could you share some insights on that because, again, in my Catholic culture it seemed to be something that happened quite remotely, at the holy end of the Church, and there seems to be a kind of philosophical understanding of transubstantiation, and again that's going back to your confreres, Aquinas and so on. It seemed to be something that agonised people, they believed this transformation or they didn't, but I know you've spoken quite differently about the Eucharist. Can you share that with us please?

TR: First, I'd say that at the core of the Eucharist are Jesus' words: "I give myself to you, totally and without reserve". The doctrine on transubstantiation, which looks so complicated, is just trying to preserve that simple truth, which is ultimately beyond our grasp: God gives himself to us utterly and without reserve. You can get it wrong in two ways: one is to say "Oh, well, giving us the bread is like a sort of symbol of giving himself" as if I were to say to you "It's been lovely meeting you and here's a book I've written as a symbol of our friendship". Transubstantiation says "No, no, no, it's much deeper than that. The Eucharist is not a mere symbol. This really is the body of Jesus." And the other way we can get it wrong is to think that when Jesus says "This is my body, I give it to you" he means it literally in the same sense that my body is sitting in this chair, but the Church doesn't teach that. People are often surprised when they learn that the Church believes that when you move the host, you can't move Jesus because he's not present in that sort of plonkingly literal way. So this wonderful doctrine moves us beyond mere symbolism and simplistic literalism. People don't have to study the doctrine of transubstantiation, all we need to know is that he truly, truly gives himself without reserve. But if you are bothered by what this means, then the doctrine is there to help you.

he truly, truly gives himself without reserve

But, to go back another stage, I think the transforming experience for me, what really helped me to see the centrality of the Last Supper, was a journey that I've often described, in Rwanda. One of the first days of the genocide, we were due to go to the north of Rwanda to see our sisters and the Belgian ambassador came and he said "Stay at home, the whole country is burning." But we were young, or younger, and foolish and we set out and were caught up in everything. It was a grim day, and that evening, when I arrived at my sisters', their house was filled with bullet marks from fighting the previous day, I said "Oh, what on earth can I say?" I couldn't think of anything to say but the Church gave me something to do, which was to remember how on the night before he died he took bread and broke it. That was the darkest moment in the history of the Church, there seemed to be no future, there was only suffering, there was only failure and in this utter pit he made a gesture of hope. "This is my body and I give it to you" and whenever we find ourselves in some pit of darkness that's when we remember what he did, the gift of an utterly inexplicable future. This is our hope. That's what I discovered that day in Rwanda.

RF: It's very powerful to reflect on the worst of human experience and yet still listening to you it seems that hope is very much alive in you and that our theme is those words from 1 Peter which are: "Give an account of the hope that's in you". You've obviously seen darkness in some of the worst excesses of the human condition and yet you seem to me to exude hope, that experience notwithstanding. So could you try and just explain why it's linked to everything we've said in some sense, can you try, in a nutshell, to explain why hope is so much more powerful than anything else for you?

TR: Whenever I've been to the darkest places I've always come back with more hope. I've spent some time in Iraq earlier this year, in Bagdad and then up in the camps in Kurdistan and I wondered what hope I could bring them. But they gave me hope. When you visit people in *in extremis,* where the superficial joys and contentment are stripped away, then you hope or you despair and what I generally found is that, with the grace of God, people discover a hope which is deeper than any I'd ever known before.

I remember another time going to Bagdad during Saddam Hussein's time and we feared a bombing raid that night. I thought it was going to be rather ironic if I were to be killed in Bagdad by a British bomb. The next morning I said to the brethren, "I didn't sleep much, I was wondering what was going to happen" and they said, "But we have lived with death for years. For us the question is no longer, "May I die tonight?" The only question is, "Will I rise from the dead"? These people have come to place the resurrection at the heart of their lives. I found that in Angola in civil war, and I'm going to Syria soon and I trust I will find it there too. The theme of the International Eucharistic Congress in the Philippines is hope. I'm going to take what I learnt from my brothers and sisters in Iraq, that's what I'm going to talk about because they taught me to hope.

they taught me to hope

RF: I'm sure that'll be a very fascinating journey to Syria. When you look at the situation globally and the rise of fundamentalism and extremism and terrible things done in the name of God – I know the Catholic Church has not been free of fundamentalism in its history, how do you view this current phase when so much of what's happening in the name of religion is perhaps causing such a backlash against religion in the West?

TR: Unfortunately, fundamentalism is a characteristic of modernity. It was at the beginning of the twentieth century in America as a Protestant reaction to scientific fundamentalism. Our society is very fundamentalist; some people are scientific fundamentalists, such as atheists like Richard Dawkins. Other people are market fundamentalists – everything can be reduced to the invisible hand of the market.

Our society is very fundamentalist

Religious fundamentalism is typically modern; it's a characteristic of the reductionism which is so common in modern culture. I don't think it's characteristic of religion as such, so much as of modernity. All these fundamentalisms try to reduce our understanding of the world to one small key. We have to offer a religion which is intelligent, reflective, reasonable, and poetic. Of course, faith transcends reason but in the Catholic tradition it doesn't contradict it and I think when people are tempted to reduce everything in one way or another to some ideology we have to stand up for the beautiful, complex intelligibility of things.

RF: You talk about modernity, what about the people of the modern age who are just not even at the first base when it comes to understanding; engaging with religion on the transcendent, is very far from their experience, far from their language. Their lives are comfortable, they're okay, they're satisfied, they live rich lives; they're artists, they read widely, they create, they're loving people but when it comes to religion it's meaningless to them. Is there a way in with that experience?

TR: I think there is. We should go to them because of what they give us. Then they may be able to accept what we can give them. At the beginning of the twentieth century there was a wonderful French Dominican called Couturier and he ran a magazine called L'Art Sacré, Sacred Art. He befriended all the great painters, people like Picasso and Braque, and when he wanted paintings for churches he asked them. They were fascinated because he did not regard them just as pagans to be evangelised, but as artists whose gifts we needed. Many of them became close to the Church in that way.

When the French Dominicans in Lyon wanted to design a new church, a priory, they said "Let's ask Le Corbusier", who was the most famous French architect in the world. Some people reacted: "But he's an atheist" and the French Dominicans replied: "It doesn't matter, he's a great architect, that's the important thing". So he became close to the brethren because the brethren became close to him and before he died in Paris and had asked to be buried in the South of France, he said: "I would like my body to rest for twenty-four hours in the Dominican church". So, again, we mustn't think of these people as problems, we have to think of them as gifts.

I think film makers have an enormous amount to give us. When I talk to the young, I often begin with films. I don't know whether you've come across *Of Gods and Men*, the film about the Tibhirine monks in Algeria, that was made by a man who didn't believe in God but he had to learn to pray so that he could make the film. He fell in love with the monks. He has given us so much. So I think that modernity, which is so rich and filled with such extraordinary people, has so much to give us, once we open our eyes and accept the gifts. Then people may accept the gift of faith.

RF: Obviously, you consider art to be a great gift. Can you just speak to that a little bit more please: the importance of art in your understanding of the world? You see it, presumably, in terms of a divine gift as well, or some part of a divine expression. Are there any particular artists or writers or poets who mean a lot to you personally?

TR: I think that when we say that we're made in the image and likeness of God, it doesn't mean to say necessarily that God has a nose and two eyes, although actually God has

we're given a share in God's immense creativity

in Jesus! It means that we're given a share in God's immense creativity. He spoke the word and it came to be. We speak words that destroy or give life, so the biggest question in morality is, "Do we speak loving, creative words to each other?" Artists have this special share in God's creativity and so a particular closeness to God. Among contemporary artists, I must confess to a great weakness for a Dominican artist called Kim En Joong, a Korean Dominican. He's a great abstract painter and his canvases are filled with light and they dazzle.

I had one in my office in Rome, which he gave me. When I took my mother in to see it, she looked at it rather sceptically and she said, "Darling, it looks like your habit after an exceptionally messy breakfast". I think we have all sorts of musicians who lift up our hearts, and they don't have to be Christians, you see. In my childhood people like the Beatles were so important. The Beatles had tremendous gifts and did we accept those gifts? Did we bless those gifts? We bring bread and wine to the altar to be blessed, do we bring music and song and poetry to be blessed?

RF: For those who are looking for resources or voices to help them understand the depth of the Christian journey, or to become adult Christians in this day and age, have you got any tips for us? Any one voice or writer or speaker or someone just to share that it would be good for us to look up to as a way to help us?

TR: Gosh, that's very personal! One person who has helped me a lot is Annie Dillard. She's an American writer, she's really a poet and a scientist and I think she has an extraordinary sense about how creation is a gift and how scientists can help us to see that. She wrote a lovely book called *Pilgrim at Tinker Creek*, which I strongly recommend. I love the poetry of Gerard Manley Hopkins, he's another great help in my life. And a text which often I find deeply helpful is from Psalm 143, "In the morning let me know your love". Because if only we knew how much we were loved, how different our lives would be, so in a way that's my prayer every morning: "In the morning let me know your love".

RF: Perhaps just some final reflections. I read quite a shocking statistic, that the percentage of those who go through the RCIA programme, who then leave within a year, is really quite high. In the United States it's about 70%, and we hear all the time that people come into the Church, but people are drifting away from the Church with sadness for various reasons. Do you have a message for those on the threshold of the Church, either on the way in or on the way out? What would your message to them be?

TR: Think of those who are instructed in our faith, received into the Church and then leave. In a way, it's quite normal. I think it's part of growing in faith that you make the great confession, you get baptised and then suddenly wonder what it's all about. Think of St Peter! At Caesarea Philippi he has his big moment, "You are the Christ, the Son of the living God", fantastic. Then he gets it all wrong and Jesus says, "Get behind me Satan." He doesn't understand about going to Jerusalem to die. He's terribly unhappy and he mucks it all up, and he seems to drift away from the Lord. It's absolutely standard and what people should see, when it ceases to make much sense and they feel plunged in doubt, is that that's part of the journey too, that's part of the deepening. Just as five months into your marriage

that's part of the journey too, that's part of the deepening

many people feel, "Oh, I've made a mistake and I'm not so sure. It's all gone", that's part of the journey.

The other thing to say is that you may be on the margins of the Church, coming in or going out, but that's fine because Jesus put the marginal people at the centre. When Thomas Merton became a Catholic he was bowled over by a phrase of a medieval theologian, Alan of Lille, who said, "God whose circumference is nowhere and whose centre is everywhere". We should love and cherish the marginal people, because they are, in a way, the centre of the Church. Their marginality is not a sign of exclusion but sometimes it's a sign of those whom we are called to embrace. You know when you make bread, which I'm sure you do often, you roll it out and you gather it in, you gather the edges into the middle and you roll it out and that's what the bread of the Church is, it's always gathering in those on the edge and putting them at the centre again and again. Sometimes you may feel a bit chilly there, but those on the edge are especially loved by God.

RF: Father Timothy, thank you for sharing that hope that is in you.

TR: Thank you very much.